Los Angeles Fires
of the Heart

Julie Bergman

-Undercover Books-

Paperback: ISBN 978-0-9644458-5-7
ebook: ISBN 978-0-9644458-6-4
Kindle: ISBN 978-0-9644458-8-8
Hardback: ISBN 979-8-9856037-4-3

Graphics and design: Julie Bergman
Author Photograph: Margie Woods

Undercover Books
www.undercoverbooks.net

Library of Congress Cataloging-in-Publication Data

Bergman, Julie.
  Los Angeles Fires of the Heart/Julie Bergman.
  Paperback
  p. cm.
  ISBN 0-9644458-5-9 ISBN 978-0-9644458-5-7
  1. Title.
PS3552.E71935L67 1995   811".54
                                               QBI94-2666

Manufactured in the United States of America
First Printing: January 1995 Second Printing: December 2020 Third Printing: January 2022

For my mother and father

CONTENTS

Prologue	3
Outside the Hunt	4
Changes	5
Again	6
Steel Trap	7
Celtic Unrest	8
Head Shy	9
Unharmed	10
Dance	12
Gera	14
Edinburgh	15
Equus	16
101 North to Casitas Pass	18
Imposters	19
Storm Warnings	20
Six Point Six and Counting	21
60's Baptism	22
Ventura	23
Neutral Zone - Portugal	24
Concealed Weapon	25
Mousework	26
Inside	29
Santa Barbara	30
Rain Storm	31
Witness	32
Solice	34
Shadow Man	35
Common Ground	36
Negotiations	37
Scotland	38
Imminence	39
Future Shock	40

Wolf   41
Weather   42
Interlude   43
A Different Listening   44
Windsong   45
Libations   46
White Heat, Wild Hooves   47
Mythics   49
Begin Again   50
Elements   52
Cambridge   53
Traveler   54
Gale Rising   55
Shock Waves   56
Sailor   57
Time Zones   58
Diane   59
Contact   60
Roads of the Spirit   61
Muse   62
Full Contact   64
Harmony   65
Epilogue

Los Angeles Fires
of the Heart

PROLOGUE

In a metropolis wedged between canyon and mountain,
Cluttered with promises
Of a fierce and flagging western cloth;
The surrounds are branded with an imbalance that
Sweeps like a hawk from street, to hearth, to heart.

In the mixed light within the confluence of motion,
I am a quiet set of eyes;
On a delicate and unannounced passage,
From search, to vision, to images.
On a journey, a study of players.

OUTSIDE THE HUNT

In the greenness and the air,
The fabric of a soft summer afternoon.
Struggling with the restraints of words.
Struggling with the lines on my hand.
A light wind shakes up so much emotion.

The vivid deep hills of a decade ago,
Of a rural European stream-side journey.
I went off to find definition.
Knife-sharp recall. I'm not desert born.

Wandering into the language.
Time-wise and unburdened.
Willing, and beyond the day's restrictions.

Lost in the feeling of the coming evening.
Lost over the words I'm unable to find.
Outside the quiet rhythms of earth and water,
Air and fire.
A need for depth beyond the steel,
Beyond the rigid thoughts going up in rapid
Succession, street-wise from here.

To keep death at call or at bay.
To be on the beguiling end.
Outside the hunt.
Against the grain.

CHANGES

I remember an afternoon in Cambridge. 1979.
"So you're going to La?" Patty asked me.
That was one way of looking at it, I thought.
She's a singer. It's one note on a do-re-me scale
to her.
A frenetic city to me.
A long way from where we stood.
Somewhere I never imagined I'd be.
"Yes, I'm going."

Since I arrived I've been writing about the desert
versus the forest.
I can count every stake in my soul since then, and
every touch of warmth another has given me, categorized in
terms of brittle sage
or rain-green grass.

I was sucked dry inside before I'd ever landed.
Then rehydrated, slowly,
in spite of the desert.
Finding sustenance.
My own source.

AGAIN

As still as stone.
In the quiet morning. Trying to
face up and finding the enveloping
calm inching its way around one's
sides and through one's hair.
I can feel the early morning here
and in a hundred places.

Seven quiet nights.
To write again for the sake of
forming the perfections of thought
that painfully etch their way round
and round this chasm of turnings.
For I don't know what reason.

I will put it down as before. I'd
forgotten. Now I remember.
Three o'clock in the morning after
some rather difficult days,
and now I remember.

STEEL TRAP

L.A. is a steady drone,
air and land,
by day, by night.
Freeways contingent with movement
soften but keep a grip
at evening.
Hills seal in the air
at dawn.
Stopping, stultifying.
A reminder of palms
claimed by desert,
humans staled by enclosure,
glass and steel.
A life of white noise,
suspending, freezing,
blanketing pain,
voiding memory of green,
of silence.

CELTIC UNREST

Mischievous unrest.
An unyielding May-month leading to
a henchman June.
Why am I here and not in Wales,
in its green arms?
This rocking, compelling city,
almost aesthetically barren
were it not for my peace-keeping associates,
and the ingratiating equines
who steal my attention daily.

We're some of us outlaws.
Not watching the clock.
Not in bad company, impassioned in this
impetuous world.

I'm not feeling desperate for anything
this late spring, except perhaps to see again
the green isles.

HEAD SHY

Looking for tenderness in the
passing spectrum of humans.
A selection of values and understanding.
Hesitating to say I love and need
beyond the day's close.
Music or motion,
timeless and engendering.
I'm watching you.
Fighting with the imbalance of pain.
Daring only to say take from me.
Trying not to say give to me.

UNHARMED

It's a crashing sea inside of me
or it's a deep warmth.
I can stand here quietly with
all this caring I feel.
Too much to show.
I have some truths of my own.
I love those I can
with all I can.

Within the grey confines of a
thought crowded city.
A desert city.
I have love inside of my own,
undiminishable, it has been given to me,
given back from me.

DANCE

I've been in fire and in trouble,
held now by what quiet and
warmth I can find.
Held up above the white emotion's river.

Life can be soft or harsh or balanced
and in motion like a dance.

Across these tough city highways,
souls are forgotten or fighting.
There is rough on their faces
or a smile hidden way inside.

Life is soft or harsh or daring
and moving like a dancer.

Stalking a chill morning on the outskirts
of a foreign town in a chill mood.
I've been shaken to the roots
by the stark green hills.

I've traded a strength inside for
a greater sensitivity.
How is it you forgo peace in order
to be touched so easily.

Life can be soft or harsh or quiet
and moving with a dancer's motion.

I'm inspired by their laughter,
those with lighter visions than I.
I'm down a chance street in the
confines of an idea.

Better to be moving, changing.
Finding the balance so life can move
like a dance.

GERA

From the Ides of March to the Ides of May,
I've been staring into these conclusions.
I don't wish to leave those I need.

Now in the settling gray evening,
I couldn't excuse your leaving us.
No one else was to get killed, you said,
after one of us lost to the Pacific sea.

Your husband called to tell me,
you died on my birthday.
It sent this friend in a blind fury
to the riverbank.

I walked on the dike in a gripping chill.
We were all supposed to keep together, you said.
It left this friend staring and fragile
by the quietly moving water.

You've brought around the tenderness we
have for each other,
in this circle of hearts.

From the Ides of March to the Ides of May,
I've come to these conclusions.
We don't have to leave those we need.
You have our love always.

EDINBURGH

It has been a hot few desert weeks and
I haven't been able to think very well.
The reservoirs inside haven't been there.

Not like on a cool evening in Edinburgh,
with the smell of the wet streets
mixed with the pervasive strains of the breweries,
heightened by every pub you walked by.

There is so much force to the memories that
I can feel it all the more now for not
having the abstractions of the times.

The rain and streets and dark nights
draw me back.
In my memory of it I am held
and I require it again.
I must return and be alone with my vision
until I've settled with it.

It rains in Los Angeles now.
It takes me back and hurts and soothes both.

EQUUS

In the open ended mortal game
Of trying and giving, seeking and vying,
A day or weeks of human contention end
In the dusk of a quiet evening,
On the back of 16 hands of grace
Tied to hoof and mane.

The power begotten of hock and stifle,
Fluid shoulders, tendon over bone.
The rider's asking, the horse's granting;
Pushing, yielding, gaits into rhythm.
A vision between the rider's
Hand and leg and heart.

Inspired to passion once again
By the horse spirit,
A human being given asylum
From the stark temporal realm,
Reprieved and freed
By the horse dance.

101 NORTH TO CASITAS PASS

In a Victorian sea house
North of the fuming city.
Out of the grips which
Sink lead into vision.

Off battle grounds
A pact renewed.
A longer call
Asking different movement,
Deeper sound.
Closer to heart response.

Essence.
Bring it out,
Write it down,
Give it form.

IMPOSTORS
L.A. Riots May 1992

We're ignoring the spark that
released the fires,
we've held no consensus
except that life feels pain.

The implosion of human needs
and denial burns within,
the black skies without
are giving power to rage.

This urban mass of lights
and darkness,
engenders more fear than comfort
as we deny our common humanity.

We've ignited the spark
that feeds the fire
with our images held out,
playing the strong part.

But we're behind the flames
in embers,
ready to fall
into each other's arms
at the slightest passion.

STORM WARNINGS

In a thrashing wind, under a sky of motion,
what's inside of me clamors like a burst storm.
What is tearing around at soul level
is clawing its way into the open.

I must have you, I can't find you.
I know you and I can't be without you.
Is it just the warmth I had beside you?
Every ambiguous gaze I meet asks the question,
and I have endless queries for the masses.
I can't ask each one.
I will ask you if I can find you.
I will ask you.
Will you stay?

SIX POINT SIX AND COUNTING
January 17, 1994

At the edge of a precipice that cracks and
rolls, and pierces down into the dark;
overlooking the blanket of lights that
becomes a city at dusk, and
vanishes when the lights fail.

We become a ribbon of motion
in a mirror image to the underworld,
the innerworld,
at the mercy of unseen gods.
There is no permanence here,
No standing structures immune to movement.
No hearts or emotions devoid of change.

Whenever the earth moves now
I look up and I wait,
to see where I will exist
in relation to it.

'60s BAPTISM

I wanted to be rocked,
held and rocked,
rocked by emotion.

Days were live-wired,
confusions that swore
on dark black waters and reaches.

Wine bottles and hash,
sounds and motions at variance,
music that blared fevers.

Pulsing nights in the Village,
flights to England,
measuring the beat tide.

Flirting with the ace of spaces,
sharp edges and pills,
caution abandoned.

Grasping the fierce rhythms of emotion,
asking to be rocked,
by explosions.

VENTURA

Holding fast to a rocky Pacific coast
with Dutch courage
from exuberance inside.
Watching the dichotomy this night
of the violent sea that meets
a sweet evening.

The sea is unforgiving and I am not.
It's thievish and not gentle.

The moon is complete over this ocean
as the calm increases in me
and I return to the road in the soft air.

NEUTRAL ZONE - PORTUGAL

Cliff side monastery ruins visible from the harbour.
Sand roads that twisted above the sea.
Cafe au lait served in a glass at a dockside cafe.
Long train rides up the coast to the casino town
Known during the war as an espionage centre,
A neutral zone for spies of all sides.

Horseback through the hilly Spanish like land
Above the beach town.
Late evenings alone at the very bow, at sail,
Watching the ship's motion, the night's form.
I left the country.
A year later the government fell.

I worked for everyone.
Selfless and selfish.
I want to hold pen to paper.
I want to make a difference to a few people's lives
That make a difference.

CONCEALED WEAPON

L.A. is an excuse to carry.
Scarce on these streets is a license to care.
There are multitudes of views
Along the dry white line of freeway,
Hampering my understanding
Of what sets off the snare.

Rare clouds break across the foothills,
Promising relief from the unending heat.
I'm taking pills so I can think
In the morning,
Tearing my soul so I can write
About needs.

I have yesterday that keeps disappearing
Further behind,
And moments searing inside for release.
I'm holding onto others for balance,
And hiding my weakness
From those who might see.

Intensity dominates this undertaking
With risks I can barely perceive.
The rain sounds like clapping and laughter,
The future is a danger surrounding me.

MOUSEWORK

Banished to a residential den,
From freedom to hunt in endless barn aisles.
Confined to a lesser estate.
A cat removed.

The house is mouse-barren,
No work to be done.
A rare bug interrupts the stillness,
But for that other cat;

Grey and hunched large,
Around the corner or in the hall.
Unwelcoming and on guard
In the larger chambers.

During the long afternoons,
The Grey creeps around its rooms,
Bold but unsure;
Not a dare, but a hiss.

The displaced hunter sits crouched
Or curled white on the windowsill.
Listening between naps in the day,
Careful for a chance at night;

Awaiting an escape past the Grey sentinel,
Out the door, back to the stable,
Where the bugs and mice
Run rampant by now.

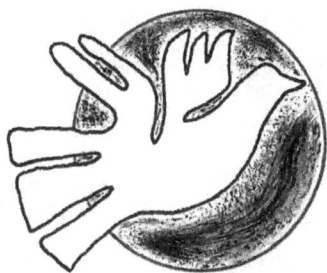

INSIDE

My heart is a balance scale,
Measuring out how much,
How little.
Increments of grace,
Cups of emotion.
I'm made of delicate visions
That weaken, strengthen,
Within metered phases.
Bursting full,
Or depleted, nearly invisible.
Gauging the reach,
The receive.
Fractions of tender,
Traded many times over.
Bartered caring for caring,
To find equilibrium
Beyond the fragile.

SANTA BARBARA

Fighting immotion and the ragged edges
of a summer morning,
beneath the mist and the coast hills.

Resting back up against the beach rocks,
trying to find a strength at all.

I do not know what there is here to hold.
I am not set to this shore and sea.

All I know is that what I can give,
I give from my heart,
and that I am honour bound.

RAIN STORM

The streets are empty with the fallen rain
and I'm walking to the river with
a mile between us.
Ten hours later and I'm searching
in the white surf,
for the feeling of touching you,
and swallowing your liquid eyes.

Does the feeling of darkness ever leave?
I want to feel that I am not meant
to feed the seething tide.

WITNESS

Balancing the motion.
A black woman bus driver
Moving down her empty aisle and dancing,
Waiting for the green.

A blue trimmed beach house
With two silver cars,
His and hers matched loans and dreams
Covering up their differences.

Balancing the incoming waves.
Midnight immigrant fishers
Hanging their thoughts over the pier,
Waiting for a tug, a pull, a wish.

A man on wheels
With a child on wheels.
A woman holding her blond haired birthright,
Laughing in a mother's voice.

Balancing fingers and nails.
Someone in slow motion
Walking along the Pacific Sea.
My lesson, my creation, my eyes.
Passing through the heatwave,
The coldspell, the changes.

Fingering music and writing my name,
Skipping stones a fraction ahead of time.

Balance me, balance me.
I'm praying in circles,
Engulfed season after season
Or reprieved from the riptide.

I'm watching myself and others
Casting our designs.

SOLACE

Bending too many layers of necessity
Around too little presence of mind.

A crashing demand for evolution,
Seeking me out in portions,
Tearing me, bits at a time.
Feeding pieces back to keep
My hunger alive.

A legacy of uncertainty,
Accompanying me
From one encounter to the next,
One dinner table to the next,
One uneasy solitude
To the next.

Going lighter on the perfection,
Letting the universe come to me.
Giving out solace,
Accepting tomorrow as the messenger
Of seasons.

SHADOW MAN

One whose touch was unselfish warm,
whose care reminded me of something earlier.
Reasoning true to reason,
native as sand to desert region.

Beside me,
I'm tracing shadows.
I've a stomach clutching fear,
now given to more gentle reminders.

COMMON GROUND

A cat night
In a foothill town,
With a freeze in the air
And a light wind talking up dead leaves.
The cats have their own business
Orchestrated house to yard to private place.
Blithe shadows glancing off the pavement.
Nearly soundless transactions,
Clandestine purposes.
Indifferent to other reasons,
My reasons
For frequenting the same piece of darkness,
The same acre of suburban high desert.

A cat's theatre,
Progressing at a rhythmic pace
Unmindful of my passage,
Their mirror image.
I've the same mission but less grace
Moving scene to scene,
Intrigue to quiet intrigue.
But we stop and eye each other
Mid-street
Long enough to heed the reflection.

NEGOTIATIONS

Whatever I can tell you
In some halting description,
Piecemeal.
It's insufficient.
The malcontentment
That pushes me canyon to sea
Says yes and no,
Go and wait.
I'm forever a mediator.
I've a vague knowing
There's more outside.
Someone or some place imagined
Should I only look further,
Testing not for ease
But for the chase,
The break in the canyon.
To erase the discomfort of inaction,
Outwit the loneliness that
Stalks out of sight.
I've a place inside me
That I've come to live with
By paying graft
To this highwayman.

SCOTLAND

Never lost to me shall you be,
though the five and thousand miles
lie as a fallen bridge between us.

There are mighty hills in Scotland.
They rise as kings,
and never a sheer fall between them.

The coast as may be seen,
never to a frail heart be comfort,
the plains and desert sands
are one to thee.

But jagged coast though you see,
a witness to the blazing waters,
the cliffs stand and yonder do I.

IMMINENCE

Emotion is a quiet rider
coming to me like part of the earth.
The future is a quiet motion
I'm surprised to have survived.

FUTURE SHOCK

Days lie across the frozen suspense
of my imagination,
measured in written increments,
judged by action or inaction.

Time started early in a pine forest
surrounding my confusions,
and ended yesterday in the city
or wherever I last put mind to ink.

I'm serious about emotion,
about trading danger for pain;
having a catalyst for motion,
a reason for belonging.

I'm playing with half a memory
but a complete heart;
visited by longing,
wounds I can't find.

The future shows like a soft mist
shrouding all chance of knowing.
I have complex needs and expectations.
I meet it running.

WOLF

At the cornerstone of a weathered ruins,
I stand facing the elements, fragile and burdened;
burning from the damp cold on the brae.

I wrap needs around me like a cloak,
as a futile buffer against being alone
on the long course down the hillside.

Lost between believing and not believing
in a future, pain tracks me like a wolf
across the storm-swept moor.

WEATHER

Waiting for an edge and a break
from the intermittent, smoldering clouds
that are unremitting,
when they reach and settle into me.

I am no longer frozen and motionless,
but it still moves up from behind
and touches,
to remind that respite is tentative.

I have to fight still,
for breath.

INTERLUDE

You close up like a flower
drawing its petals up
when the night threatens.
Those who know of
the delicate beauty inside
wait for you
until the air is mild and gentle,
and the mists renewing,
until you feel the sun's warmth again
and stretch out your petals
one by one.

A DIFFERENT LISTENING

The moon is rising headlong
into a wooded night.
The forest is listening
to sounds that issue
from my internal damage.
There is anguish with a birthright
in flora and fauna,
gripping like a tree's implacable search
for sustenance,
suffering from ill placed roots.
Or the confusion of a wood animal
on an asphalt road,
the inexplicable reality that claims
slow victims.
Do I move, do I freeze?
If I be still and part of the night,
will I be taken down by other's intentions?

I'm going deep into the redwoods
to be still,
one of earth's creatures
with a simpler pain
and a forest to listen.

WINDSONG

Far hills call me on,
Near seas find me.
Songs of time bind my heart,
Tender mercies free me.

LIBATIONS

Suspended within some ragged emotions
That toss and lurch
With comings and goings,
But leaving me a full complement
Of inner relations.
A higher exchange.

I didn't really know I'd never
Been much given to,
Until I found myself drinking up
This latest reality.
I'm finally being served an energy
To match my expenditure.

How could I have been so arrogant
As to not allow others
To contribute to me, you asked.
Well...alright then,
Pour me another.

WHITE HEAT, WILD HOOVES

The white heat that tears into me
Like a wild horse's hooves,
Unrestrained, ungrieved.
I am not surrendered, not withheld,
But jettisoned into the fury,
A cougar against a flailing stallion.

Not fractions, not piecemeal,
Wholesale, pouring deliverance.
Strength feeding strength,
A master and a master,
In a mutual fearless
Spiritual bidding.

The hot dust subsides.
Horse and human stare at
Undamaged spirits and torn hides.
By duplication of force,
Natural selection has given us both
A wild heart.

MYTHICS

The white moon in the black night,
A white mistress, baited and bribed,
Illuminating the hills.

Courier horsemen dispatched on mission,
As ravens carrying berry and seed,
Seeking the quintessence.

Messengers on a sovereign's plea,
Tracing the grail's engravings,
Painted by breath of sky.

Ahead in the mists,
In the suspended grey,
Imprinted in chalk on the cliff face;

The designs of spirit,
The metered pulse of heart,
Demarking time, bearing fruit.

BEGIN AGAIN

I don't bring resolve to
this vision,
only impetus to the cutting wind,
to the differing pattern.

Yesterday I was here.
Today I am here now.
Finding a loose chain, a
break in stride.

Like a horse,
I change my mind slowly,
but I'm celebrating new
thoughts like a birthday.

A stop in mediocrity.
A break in the inattention along
the highway,
where others wait.

They all hang, sometime.
Waiting for a meal,
for a job,
for a miracle.

When I remember the sounds
that opened my eyes,
I know the thunder and beat,
the time coming.

Hot and colder, it all
comes with the music,
with relief
in the skies.

I'm driven to the
song that burns.
I can ache like part of the earth,
trespassed.

Instead, I heed the weather
that shapes the tides.
And watch others try and
avoid the blues.

They line up
all along the boulevard,
waiting for a miracle,
for the day to begin.

ELEMENTS

The gusting wind
that tears and heaves
the trees in their sleep
takes as much from me.

The unsettling currents
circling the hillside
pit me against my own
uneven sleep,
vulnerable to
deeper stirring.

I didn't intend to find
such unrest,
when mining for portions of myself
that denied exposure
to touch and air.

The turbulence gives way
to a false calm,
only to be buffeted
by another chilling storm front
as the night destroys patterns
inside and out.

CAMBRIDGE

Some things are consistent.
The same voices that filled me
Twenty years ago.
Harvard's acoustics
Or Berklee's reeds,
Or Dublin's soulman in Boston,
Smokey cellar real. Up
Close to the sax.
Sliding off steel strings.
I was 16 on the Commons,
Or 20 in the Square.
We're older and the same.
Visions, still near enough.
Appearing again.
To give me a stinging flash
Of my beginnings.
My road
Close to the singers.
Something we felt then
Is still new, unfailing.
I'm so happy
To still need you.

TRAVELER

Dreams,
Seeking me,
Finding me against some other backdrop,
Holding me close,
Freeing me to see other content,
Other colour.

I have destroyed a repetition,
Shattered a holding pattern,
Burst into motion-making sound.

Fascination,
Winning me,
Handing me another season,
Daring me to give another round,
Another reason.

I know more than before about losing,
Less about standing still,
More about moving.

GALE RISING

Pushed on and awake by the fleet star
that surfaces easterly, relentlessly.
Forcing me again into the dawn stream.
Wide eyed I am still,
at what I craft.
The reasons for believing lie
futile or absent,
or rushing gale force like humanity.
In the face of being
I am intrigued and vulnerable.
I wish for some to need me more.
One with a slice of passion
for my survival.

SHOCK WAVES

Slightly to the left of reality,
Courage notwithstanding,
Fear marks time and brushes against
What I keep in reserve.

I'm trying for a middle road,
Zealots on one side,
Cynics opposed to the greater good
Gathered opposite.

There is a warmth of reason,
It reaches me and deserts me,
Alternately shaken, shaken but
Reason having the last word.

There are inner dialogues
Between self and past, self and future,
Gathering in a storm of abstracts with
Shock waves beating a path to yes.

If I can save honour to the last
I will go on willingly,
The next life-defining stage
As welcome as morning.

SAILOR

The wave pulls me in all directions.
Ideas grasping one side and
emotion tearing the other.
I'm spilling, hurting, searching,
then stopped dead still.
Caught by a man's quiet eyes
I suddenly wish to know,
to give to.

My life is suddenly at streamside or in
ocean port.
I'm at dock temporarily.
I keep finding you and losing
you in other people.
Won't you put out a beacon?

TIME ZONES

A soft sky over the clouds,
azure and yellow at the
horizon,
across the East
relinquishing desert,
absolving the drought
into green.

A hydrating flight
sliding like a blues bar
across guitar strings,
oblivious to patterns.

Wide and open
escaping definition.
The skyline
vanishing into evening,
time zones away.

DIANE

Letting the body down slowly,
Signing off the finite
With grace,
Porous with future,
Expressions of more
Sunrises and exchanges,
Enveloping storms
And peace.

All the people who can only talk
About your struggle,
They miss the point.
You reinvent your will
Whenever life calls for it.
Not chasing ghosts,
But beckoning light
And reversing fortunes.

What motivates you isn't what
Pulses through veins,
But your intense direction,
Bringing others
To match your passion.

CONTACT

Hills and mist.
I don't think of the war tonight.
I feel the strains of color
That find me.
The light, dark,
Saxophone lines.
The softened edges
Of a single-reed instrument.
Glimpses of forest,
Of marsh.
I think of the curved-neck wildfowl
Who watched me today
As I drifted beside them
On the current.
Human driftwood
Beneath white clouds.

I won't be measured.
I'm reached by points of light
On a proportional scale
Of infinity,
Beginning in the hills and mist,
Or on some waterfront
As still as sound.

ROADS OF THE SPIRIT

I took ten years to fulfill
an adventure of the spirit,
and ten years to unwind
the fears that came unbidden
with others' answers.

Inside is a less complex being
with greater freedom
from knowing a counterbalance
between earth and sky,
seeking and giving.

I'm not now trying to measure
the cosmic pieces
and the equanimity of time
by the lines on my sword
or the things in my hand.

In these lives that pass like minutes,
I've come to know a truer scale.
Whosoever judges me
will be one
whose heart has held mine.

MUSE

According to chance
and according to plan,
the dawn to dusk stream of thoughts
and words, and others
engages me.

In the struggle to reconcile what is never
and what is,
I reach the edge of the hills
and walk with heather under my feet,
above the scree fallen from the cliffside.

The green entrenchments lie
above the white-grey city and
the hot, shattered streets;
separate from the agonized mediocrity
that settles on the lower valley.

Across the blue clean air,
locked in a bounding, cascading rhythm
that shakes and toils, and wakes me more.
I'm giving notice to the earth's keeper;
I won't agree, I don't agree.

Like a flood dam burst high up,
sentencing the valley,
sentience has gripped me.
Words, like so much bargaining power,
no longer evade me.

I grant the visceral hold
of the muse.
Like border-controlled
thought immigration,
I mete out my assentions.

It's a glorious dousing;
a reflection of light off the tiny slices
of granitestone and mica.
A tender slip of water though grass blades,
mercury-fluid in its passage.

May the gods soothe me
so I can contain it;
listen to me
so I can play it.
Whatever is shaking, pursuing, animating me.

Driving me to the fertile hillsides
above the scree.

FULL CONTACT

Like the undulating waves
Or the flight of sea birds,
We ebb and surge,
Reaching for our own strength.

The heart finally seizes the transition
And grants that peace can co-exist
With the tides,
With the changes.

There is challenge in waking,
In breathing,
In seeing,
In walking onto empty beaches
And being still,
Facing the calm
Or the turbulence
With open eyes.

HARMONY

There is a quiet, broad solo
Evolving from minor cosmic scales
To major chords.
Unconsonant, conflicting powers,
Drifting into God-like harmonic refrains.
Back and forth,
Following some uncharted melodic pattern.
Unmindful of the beat of humankind;
Of the soothing touches,
The harsh pain,
The giving of freedoms,
Or wearing of bonds.

Behind my eyes, I watch life sway
From the safe and familiar chorus
To the frightening unknown.
In between,
Playing out the spiritual lines
In the universe's half-way zone.

It's not a true world.
There are only true hearts,
That need constant care
To resolve the counterpoint.

EPILOGUE

I am impatient now when I can't feel gentle
and when I cannot learn fast enough.
When there is some rough edge in me I
don't want drawn for anyone.

What I thought I knew keeps changing.
But if I have nothing else,
I've had much,
and I won't be careful this gentle evening.

A NOTE ABOUT THE GRAPHICS

Front matter: A design derived from the inscriptions on a Viking rune stone, thought to be carved by Stockholm artist, Arbjorn, circa 1080 AD. The historic monument is located on farmlands in Skramsta, Sweden, owned by a descendant of the author's great, great paternal grandfather.

Pg. 17 The Chief of the Norse gods, Odin, and his eight-legged charger, Sleipnir, adapted from a jewelry motif by Shetland Silvercraft.

Pg. 66 The Japanese character depicting the ancient principle of ki. In the study of Aikido, a modern non-violent Japanese martial art, ki represents the basic, creative force in life, which transcends time and space. Aikido has as its goal the unity of ki-mind-body.

A NOTE ABOUT THE AUTHOR

Julie Bergman lived and worked in Boston and Cambridge until emigrating to Los Angeles, where she became involved in the music business, wrote feature articles for magazines, and traveled regularly to the British Isles and Ireland. She began her career as a licensed detective in 1987. She continues to work as a private investigator, with a specialty in finding missing persons and environmental investigations. She is the author of *The Finder, Poems of a Private Investigator, Ireland's Daughter, The Life and Times of Actor Sheelagh Cullen,* and the mystery novel, *Grieving Ground.*

www.ingramcontent.com/pod-product-compliance
Lightning Source LLC
Chambersburg PA
CBHW031632040426
42452CB00007B/786